948
M

Martell, Hazel Mary

Over 900 years ago

$13.95

DATE			
APR 2 1F			

007154   9033974

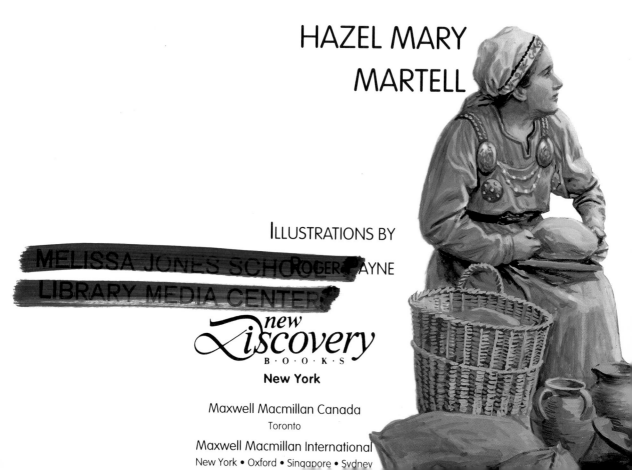

OVER 900 YEARS AGO

WITH THE VIKINGS

HAZEL MARY MARTELL

ILLUSTRATIONS BY
ROGER PAYNE

new
Discovery
B·O·O·K·S
New York

Maxwell Macmillan Canada
Toronto

Maxwell Macmillan International
New York • Oxford • Singapore • Sydney

First American publication 1993 by New Discovery Books, Macmillan Publishing
Company, 866 Third Avenue, New York, NY 10022
Maxwell Macmillan Canada Inc., 1200 Eglinton Avenue East, Suite 200, Don Mills,
Ontario M3C 3N1

Macmillan Publishing Company is part of the Maxwell Communication Group of
Companies

First published in Great Britain by Zoë Books Limited, 15 Worthy Lane, Winchester,
Hampshire SO23 7AB

A ZOË BOOK

Devised and produced by
Zoë Books Limited
15 Worthy Lane
Winchester
Hampshire SO23 7AB
England

Printed in Italy by Grafedit SpA
Design: Julian Holland Publishing Ltd
Picture research: Victoria Sturgess
Illustrations: Roger Payne
Production: Grahame Griffiths

10 9 8 7 6 5 4 3 2 1

Library of Congress Cataloging-in-Publication Data
Martell, Hazel.
    Over 900 years ago : with the Vikings/Hazel Mary Martell; illustrations by
Roger Payne.
        p. cm.—(History detective)
    Includes index.
    Summary: Examines the lifestyle of the Vikings and what we have learned about them
from the artifacts found in Viking settlements.
    ISBN 0-02-726325-8
    1. Vikings—Juvenile literature. 2. Northmen—Juvenile literature. [1. Vikings.]
I. Payne, Roger, fl. 1969, ill. II. Title. III. Series.
DL65.M36   1993
948'.022—dc20   93.2647

Photographic acknowledgments

The publishers wish to acknowledge, with thanks, the following photographic sources:

7 Werner Forman Archive/Viking Ship Museum, Bygdoy; 11 Statens Historiska Museum,
Stockholm; 14 Werner Forman Archive/Statens Historiska Museum, Stockholm;
19 Robert Harding Picture Library; 23,27 Ancient Art and Architecture Collection

Cover inset Antikvarisk-topografiska arkivet, Stockholm

CONTENTS

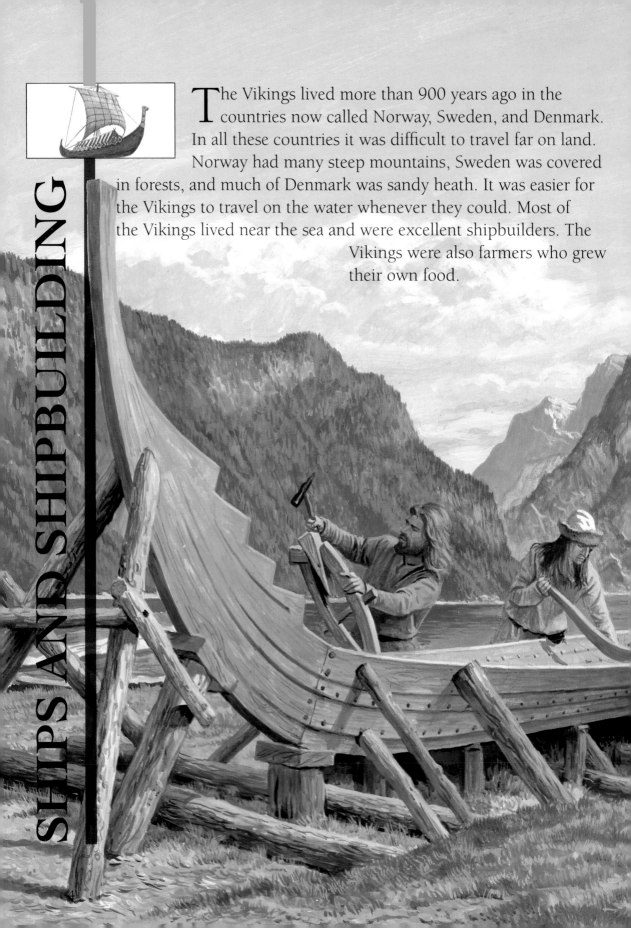

SHIPS AND SHIPBUILDING

The Vikings lived more than 900 years ago in the countries now called Norway, Sweden, and Denmark. In all these countries it was difficult to travel far on land. Norway had many steep mountains, Sweden was covered in forests, and much of Denmark was sandy heath. It was easier for the Vikings to travel on the water whenever they could. Most of the Vikings lived near the sea and were excellent shipbuilders. The Vikings were also farmers who grew their own food.

The Vikings were busy harvesting their crops in the summer and autumn. However, in winter and early spring, there was not much work to do on the farm. They often built their new ships at this time of the year. Sometimes they used a special boat shed, but usually they worked in the open air.

The Vikings used the trunk of a large oak tree to make the keel of the ship. The keel was supported on wooden stocks. The front and back posts were then nailed on to it and wedge-shaped planks for the sides were added from the bottom upward. Wooden ribs were nailed to the planks to keep the ship in shape.

On board ship

Viking ships could be sailed or rowed on rivers and lakes as well as on the sea. The ships were strong but flexible, so they did not break up in rough seas. This allowed the Vikings to travel farther than any other Europeans at that time. Some went to Iceland, Greenland, and North America, as well as western and southern Europe. Others sailed down the rivers of Russia. Some then crossed the Black Sea to what is now Istanbul. Others crossed the Caspian Sea to Baghdad.

The ax was the most important tool for the Viking shipbuilder. The shipbuilder used it to chop down trees, to split the trunks into planks for the sides of the ship, and to trim flat surfaces.

The adz was used to shape curved surfaces in large pieces of wood. These could then be smoothed out with a file until they were the right shape.

The shipbuilder used a variety of other tools for finer work. The auger (right) was used to bore holes in wood—ready for wooden pegs or iron nails. The two molding irons (left) were used to cut grooves to decorate some of the planks. Other decorations were cut into the wood with chisels and knives.

The Oseberg ship was excavated in Norway in 1904. The ship had been buried around 850 and contained everything a royal lady needed for her journey to another life. By studying this ship, people have learned a great deal about Viking methods of shipbuilding.

Each Viking ship had a big square sail woven from wool. The ships also had several pairs of oars. The number of oars depended on the length of the ship. Each ship was steered by a rudder that was like a large wooden paddle at the rear, or stern, of the vessel. At each end of the ship there was a small deck where food and drink for the journey were stored. Awnings and posts were also stored on board and used to make shelters when the ship was anchored. As it could be cold and wet on board, the Vikings stored their spare clothes in chests. They could then sit on the chests when rowing the boat. They also took sleeping bags made from animal skins. The sailors used the sleeping

The Vikings used wood to construct houses and all kinds of blocks and frames, as well as for shipbuilding. Wooden pegs were often used instead of metal nails. Tools, weapons, and cooking equipment were all made of metal, but the Vikings did not know how to produce large amounts of metal. What other reasons might they have had for using wood instead of metal? How many uses for wood can you find in the shipbuilding picture?

HISTORY DETECTIVE

bags when they had to spend the night on the open sea.

Many Vikings believed that when they died they traveled to the afterlife on a ship. Some Viking kings and queens were buried in ships with all the equipment they would need for the journey to the afterlife. Other Vikings had their graves marked with stones in the shape of a ship.

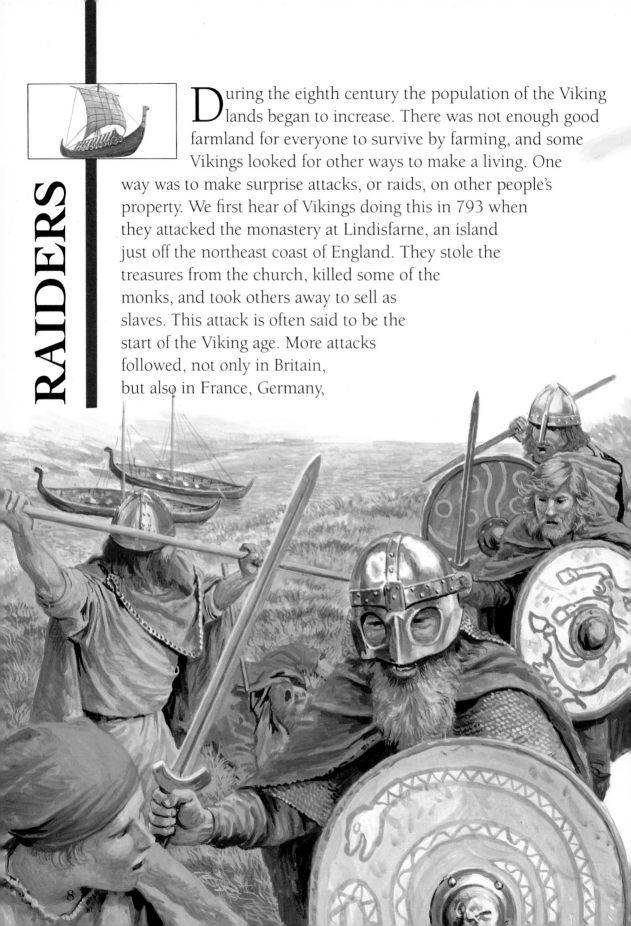

RAIDERS

During the eighth century the population of the Viking lands began to increase. There was not enough good farmland for everyone to survive by farming, and some Vikings looked for other ways to make a living. One way was to make surprise attacks, or raids, on other people's property. We first hear of Vikings doing this in 793 when they attacked the monastery at Lindisfarne, an island just off the northeast coast of England. They stole the treasures from the church, killed some of the monks, and took others away to sell as slaves. This attack is often said to be the start of the Viking age. More attacks followed, not only in Britain, but also in France, Germany,

and the Netherlands. The first targets for the Vikings were monasteries, which were often full of treasures but were poorly defended. However, as the Vikings grew more daring, they attacked towns and cities. In 834 they raided the town of Dorestad in the Netherlands. In 835 they attacked towns along the coast of Britain.

After a raid the Vikings sailed home with the goods they had stolen.

In 845 the Vikings who attacked Paris found an easier way of gaining wealth. They surrounded, or besieged, the city and refused to leave until the king gave them 6,600 pounds (3,000 kg) of silver. More Vikings began to use this tactic and the money that they were given became known as Danegeld. They kept coming back for more money, and large amounts were paid to them over the next two centuries, especially by the kings of England.

Weapons and armor

The Viking warriors who went raiding were always few in number. They relied on surprise to help them defeat the people in the towns they attacked. If the people fought back strongly, the Vikings sometimes made a wall with their shields and fought together behind it. Otherwise they fought as individuals.

The Vikings' favorite weapons were the sword and the battle-ax. They also used spears and a large knife called a scramasax. The raiders protected their bodies with wooden shields, and some wore chain-mail shirts, called birnies. Only a few of the warriors wore birnies, as they cost a lot of silver. The raiders had helmets made of iron or thick leather to protect

The Viking battle-ax was a deadly weapon. It could easily chop through shields and even through helmets.

The Vikings sometimes used spears for stabbing people. More often they threw them at the enemy at the start of a pitched battle and gathered up the spears afterward.

The Viking's favorite weapon was his sword. Its blade was made from several rods of iron, twisted together, then hammered flat and edged with steel. The handle, or hilt, of the sword was often decorated with silver or gold. Many swords had names such as "Adder" and "Leg-biter." Good swords were passed down from father to son.

Shields were usually round. They were made from flat boards of wood. The boss, or ornament, in the middle was made from iron. Some shields also had an iron rim.

If a Viking died overseas, his family might have a stone raised near his home in memory of him and his travels. This stone at Lingsberg in Sweden is in memory of a Viking named Ulvrik. It tells us that he was given two payments of Danegeld in England. In 911 the king of France found a different way of buying peace from the Vikings. Instead of paying Danegeld he gave the area we now call Normandy to a group of Vikings on condition that they help to defend France from other Viking attackers.

their heads. These helmets were sometimes decorated with patterns but did not have horns or wings attached to them.

For a long time historians knew only about the Viking raiders. This was because the only people who could read or write in Viking times were the monks. They wrote about the attacks on the monasteries and towns but not about any good things the Vikings might have done. However, people who study objects from the past, or archaeologists, have found evidence that shows the Vikings were not just violent raiders.

In the first raids the Vikings stole only whatever treasure they could find. Later, they attacked coastal towns on market days when the streets were crowded with people from the countryside, and took men and women as slaves. Some of the slaves worked for the Vikings, but most of them were sold for silver in the markets of the Middle East.

HISTORY DETECTIVE

While some Vikings became rich through raiding, others made their fortunes as traders. They sailed inland along the rivers of Europe, as well as across the open sea. By the middle of the ninth century, Vikings from Sweden had crossed the Baltic Sea to Russia, where the Slavs who lived there had begun to set up trading posts. At first the Vikings traded with the Slavs. Then they started sailing farther south along rivers such as the Volga and the Dnieper. On this journey the Vikings were always in danger of being attacked by local tribesmen. They also had to overcome the problem of long stretches of rapids on the Dnieper River. The rapids were so bad that the ships could not sail through. Instead the ships had to be lifted out of the water and carried along the bank. In spite of these

dangers, the Vikings had reached Istanbul, which they called Miklagard, by 860. Some Vikings even got as far as Baghdad. Both these places were international trading centers where goods from all parts of the known world could be bought or sold. In these cities they sold slaves for gold, jewelry, wine, and spices. They also bought silk and brocade from China. When they had bought all the luxury goods they could afford, the Viking traders set off back to the market town of Birka in Sweden.

Some of the goods were traded along the route in markets such as Kiev and Novgorod, but most went to the market in Birka. Here, the goods were exchanged or sold to traders from all over the Viking world. The traders exchanged their goods from the East for more slaves, furs, silver, wax, or honey.

Silver and glass

Archaeologists have found out about Viking traders by excavating the sites of the old market towns such as Birka; Hedeby in Denmark; Kaupang in Norway; Dublin in Ireland; and York, or Jorvik, in England. In each place the archaeologists found the remains of items that were not made locally. For example in York they found silk from China, whetstones from Norway, coins from Samarkand, and millstones from the Rhineland. However, the most exciting finds come from the graves of Viking traders in Sweden. When the traders died, their favorite possessions were buried with them. These grave goods included objects made of glass and pottery, as well as silver and jewelry. By studying where these artifacts came from, archaeologists worked out the trading links between the Vikings and the rest of the world in the early years of the Viking age. Later, however, many Vikings became Christians, and their possessions were no longer buried with them.

This glassware was found in the grave of a wealthy merchant in Birka. It was probably made in the Rhineland or in eastern Europe.

This "horn of plenty" is from the grave of a Viking man. It holds his most precious possessions. These include silver coins from different countries and arm-rings. He could wear these as jewelry or exchange them for other items.

As well as the archaeological evidence, we know about Viking trade from the sagas. The sagas are stories about great Viking adventures that were first told in the Viking age but were not written down until the 13th century. Most of the sagas are about Vikings who went to live in Iceland. Few trees grew in Iceland, which meant that there was hardly any wood for shipbuilding, but there were plenty of fish to catch. So the Vikings from Iceland traded cargoes of smoked or dried fish in exchange for wood from Britain or Norway needed to build their ships.

Viking market towns were colorful places. As well as trading centers, the markets were good places to pick up the latest gossip. Travelers brought news from all parts of the Viking world. People went to the market to buy jewelry, silverware, and other goods that they could not make for themselves at home. Many of these items have now been discovered by archaeologists. How many different items can you see being traded in the picture?

HISTORY DETECTIVE

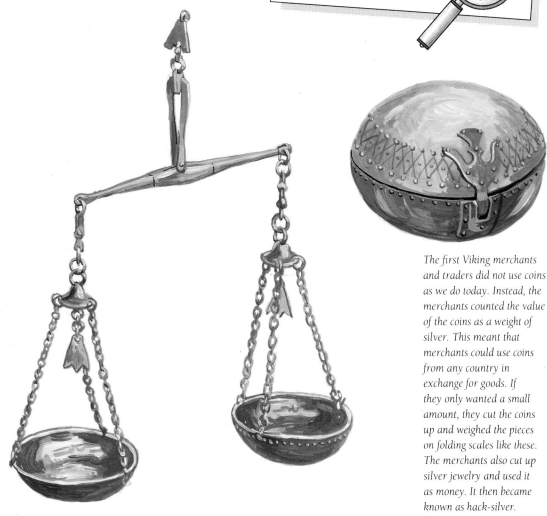

The first Viking merchants and traders did not use coins as we do today. Instead, the merchants counted the value of the coins as a weight of silver. This meant that merchants could use coins from any country in exchange for goods. If they only wanted a small amount, they cut the coins up and weighed the pieces on folding scales like these. The merchants also cut up silver jewelry and used it as money. It then became known as hack-silver.

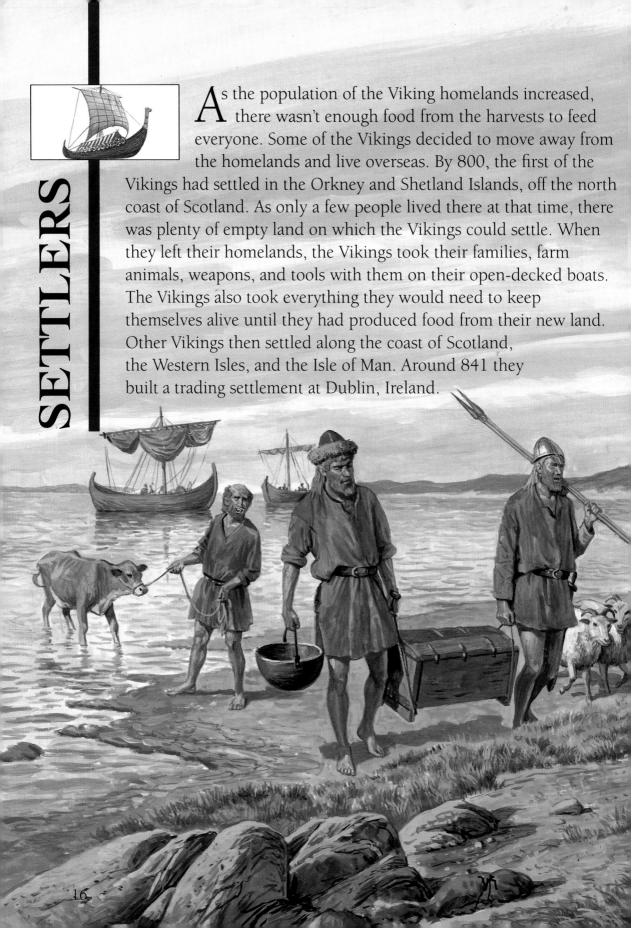

As the population of the Viking homelands increased, there wasn't enough food from the harvests to feed everyone. Some of the Vikings decided to move away from the homelands and live overseas. By 800, the first of the Vikings had settled in the Orkney and Shetland Islands, off the north coast of Scotland. As only a few people lived there at that time, there was plenty of empty land on which the Vikings could settle. When they left their homelands, the Vikings took their families, farm animals, weapons, and tools with them on their open-decked boats. The Vikings also took everything they would need to keep themselves alive until they had produced food from their new land. Other Vikings then settled along the coast of Scotland, the Western Isles, and the Isle of Man. Around 841 they built a trading settlement at Dublin, Ireland.

After 866 Danish Vikings settled in eastern England. By 886 there were so many of them that eastern England was known as the Danelaw.

Other Vikings sailed farther west and discovered Iceland around 860. By 874 the first settlers moved there from Norway. One Viking named

Erik the Red was outlawed from Iceland in 982. He went to Greenland, and in 985 other people joined him. His son, Leif, went to North America and spent a winter in Vinland. Another Viking, Thorfinn Karlsefni, went there around 1000 and stayed for three years.

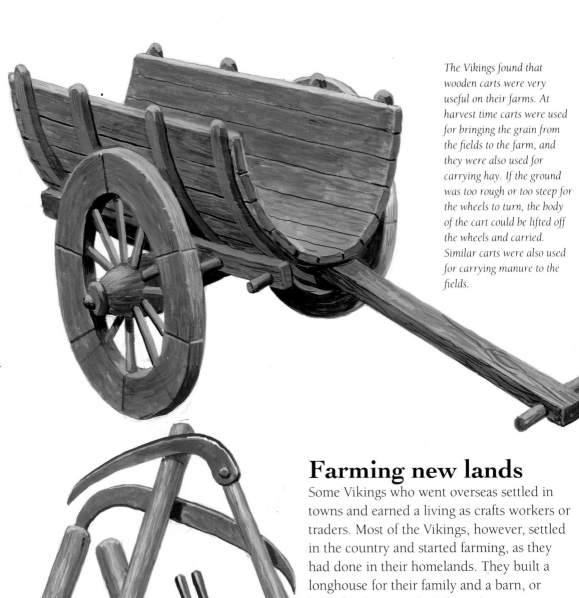

The Vikings found that wooden carts were very useful on their farms. At harvest time carts were used for bringing the grain from the fields to the farm, and they were also used for carrying hay. If the ground was too rough or too steep for the wheels to turn, the body of the cart could be lifted off the wheels and carried. Similar carts were also used for carrying manure to the fields.

Iron ore was quite plentiful in the Viking lands. Large pieces of it were often found in boggy areas. The farmers dug it up and smelted it to make tools like the ones seen here. The handles of the hammers and the sickles were made from wood.

Farming new lands

Some Vikings who went overseas settled in towns and earned a living as crafts workers or traders. Most of the Vikings, however, settled in the country and started farming, as they had done in their homelands. They built a longhouse for their family and a barn, or byre, for the animals. Where there were plenty of trees, the Vikings used wood for these buildings. Where trees were scarce, however, they used stone or even blocks of turf. They also built a smithy where they could make and mend iron tools. Near the house they grew vegetables such as onions and cabbages. They also had fields nearby where they grew grain crops such as barley and oats. These fields were walled to keep the animals out. In summer the grass was cut and dried for hay to feed the best of the animals over winter. The rest of the animals were killed for food at the end of autumn.

Archaeologists in Iceland have found enough evidence to be able to make this full-scale reconstruction of the farmhouse at Stong. The walls and the roof are made of turf.

The Vikings who settled in England mixed with the native English people. Many Viking words passed into the English language. Some of the words are still in use today, including everyday words such as bread, egg, sky, and lump, as well as place names such as Grimsby and Ravensthorpe. Many Vikings married into English families and slowly forgot their old Viking ways.

The Vikings who went to Iceland, however, kept to their old beliefs and traditions. Many went to Iceland because they wanted to be ruled by gatherings of free men, or *things*, rather than by a king. The things controlled, or governed, their local area and made laws that everyone agreed to obey. Anyone who broke these laws became an outlaw, or *nithing*, and had to leave the country.

The Vikings in Iceland also kept to their old religion until 1000. In that year they voted to become Christians. However anyone who wanted to worship the old gods in secret was allowed to do so.

How can we tell where the Vikings made new settlements? Apart from written records, there are the remains that have been dug up on ancient sites. The Vikings who went to settle in new lands often found difficulties when they first arrived. There were no shops for them to use—they had to take everything they needed with them from their homelands, including the tools they needed for building and farming. They also had to take their farm animals, along with grain to grind into flour and seeds for the next year's crops. Until the houses were built they probably set up camps, using the awnings from the ships as tents.

HISTORY DETECTIVE

The earliest Viking houses had only one room. The whole family ate and slept here. The women also did all the cooking, spinning, and weaving here, as well as bringing up the children. The room was usually oblong in shape and had a long hearth in the middle of the floor. The fire in the hearth was used to cook on and to heat the house. There was no chimney, but the smoke from the fire was supposed to go out through a hole in the roof above it. This did not always happen, and the inside of the room was often full of smoke. It was often dusty, too, as the floor was made from beaten earth. The Vikings did not have much furniture in their houses. A raised bench along each of the long walls was used for seats by day and for beds at night. There were no cupboards, but spare clothes and blankets were kept on hooks in the walls. Food was stored in barrels, jars, and tubs.

Viking Women

Women played a leading role in Viking life. As well as bringing up the children and looking after the home, they held all the keys and took charge when their husbands were away. They could marry who they wanted and also had the right to get divorced. Both women and children helped with work on the farm, especially at harvest and hay making. The women also made the family's clothes from cloth that they had dyed and woven themselves. They made tight-fitting woolen trousers and long-sleeved woolen tunics for the men and boys. The women and girls also dressed simply. They wore sleeveless woolen tunics over long pleated dresses, or shifts. These were made from linen and tied at the neck. The tunic had straps over the shoulders, held in place with brooches. In cold weather the women also wore woolen shawls.

Viking women wove on simple upright looms like this one. With the help of their children, the women spun the wool into yarn and then colored it with vegetable dyes. The dyes included woad and madder, which gave the colors blue and red. Other plants and soils gave yellow, black, orange, and green dyes.

The Vikings used metal pans for cooking, but they stored their food in wooden containers. They also used wood for their plates and spoons and for special items such as the cheese drainer (next to the ax).

Preparing food and cooking also took up a lot of the women's time each day. Rye or barley was ground in a mill to make flour for bread. Bread was baked on a flat stone slab placed over the hearth. Barley and oats were also used to make porridge. Meat was often stewed in a cauldron over the fire and vegetables such as onions and peas were added to it. Both meat and fish were sometimes baked in a pit filled with embers and covered with soil. Meat from animals killed at the beginning of autumn was salted to preserve it until spring. This meat had to be cooked with herbs and spices to hide the salty taste. The women also made butter, curd, and cheese, and beer which the Vikings drank in large amounts.

The closeness of the family was very important to the Vikings. Often children, parents, and grandparents all lived together. This could make the house very crowded, but at least there were plenty of people to share the work that had to be done. When work was finished for the day, it was time to relax by telling stories or by playing games. Clues about what the Vikings did include board games and musical instruments.

HISTORY DETECTIVE

Viking houses rarely had windows and so the fire in the hearth was used for light as well as heat. The fire was the center of family life, as this reconstruction from York shows.

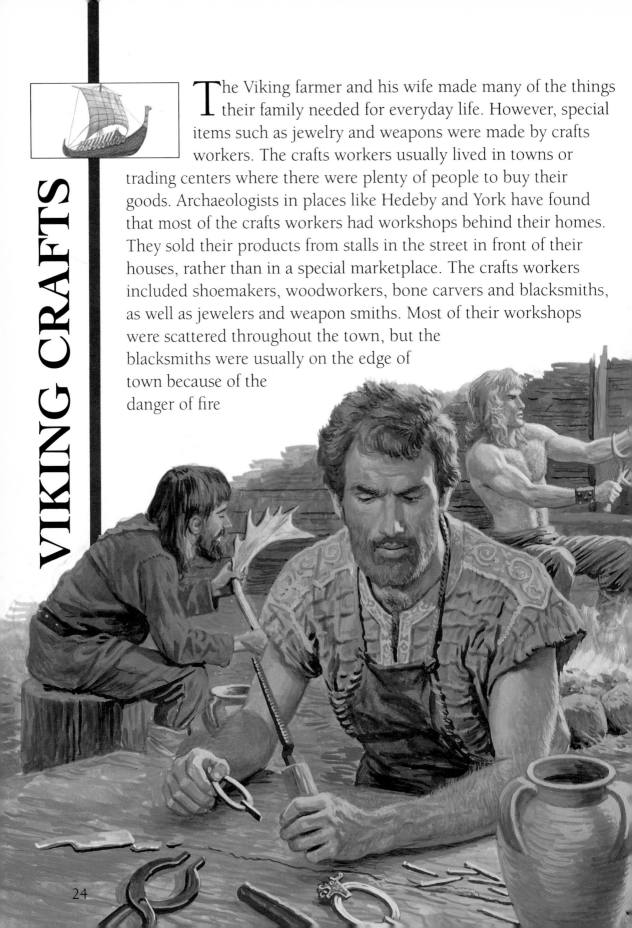

VIKING CRAFTS

The Viking farmer and his wife made many of the things their family needed for everyday life. However, special items such as jewelry and weapons were made by crafts workers. The crafts workers usually lived in towns or trading centers where there were plenty of people to buy their goods. Archaeologists in places like Hedeby and York have found that most of the crafts workers had workshops behind their homes. They sold their products from stalls in the street in front of their houses, rather than in a special marketplace. The crafts workers included shoemakers, woodworkers, bone carvers and blacksmiths, as well as jewelers and weapon smiths. Most of their workshops were scattered throughout the town, but the blacksmiths were usually on the edge of town because of the danger of fire spreading from their furnaces.

All the Viking crafts workers used natural materials. Among the most useful materials were bone and antler. The bones came from animals that had been butchered, while the antlers were collected in the woods each year after they were shed by the deer. The foot bones of cattle and horses were smoothed and used as ice skates. Other bones were made into needles, while antlers were used for making combs and buckles.

Jewelry

The jeweler was one of the most important crafts workers in Viking times. This was partly because all the Vikings liked to wear a lot of jewelry to show how rich they were. Most of this jewelry also had a practical purpose, however, as the Vikings needed some of it to fasten their clothes together. For example, both men and women used brooches to fasten their cloaks in cold weather. Women also wore two brooches to hold their tunics together and another brooch with a chain attached to it. They hung items such as keys, a knife, a needle case, and a comb on this chain, as there were no pockets in their clothes. Rich people wore brooches of

The Vikings were said to be proud of their appearance. In England the local men complained that Viking men were more popular with women than they were because the Vikings washed and combed their hair so often. This is probably true, as combs like these have been found in all the places where the Vikings settled.

silver or gold, which were made especially for them. Because these were very expensive, poor people could not afford them. Instead, poor people wore brooches made from cheap metal, such as lead, which were covered in tin to make them shine like silver. Sometimes crafts workers sold small items of jewelry to merchants, who then took them to sell at distant farms.

Viking men wore belts around their tunics. They could then suspend their sword or a knife from it in a scabbard. The belt buckle was often made from bone or antler. The buckle was often engraved with a pattern and sometimes colored with dye.

This jewelry was found in the grave of a wealthy Viking woman in Birka. The two oval-shaped brooches were the ones she used to fasten her tunic. They were known as tortoise brooches because they were shaped like tortoises. She would wear a string of beads between them. Sometimes the beads were made from silver, but they were more likely to be made from colored glass. The Vikings imported the glass in small pieces from Germany and Italy, but made the beads themselves. Some were plain, but others were many different colors.

As well as having decorative patterns on them, some Viking objects have words written on them in runes. Runes are sticklike letters that the Vikings used as an alphabet. They are sometimes known as *futhark* after the first six runes. There were only 16 of them to represent all the sounds in the language, and so writing with them was very difficult. Sometimes these runes have helped archaeologists to recognize Viking artifacts in faraway places. This in turn has helped archaeologists build up a picture of Vikings as skilled crafts workers, traders, and settlers as well as being the violent raiders the monks wrote about in the Viking age.

Before the Vikings became Christians, they worshiped their own gods. The most important was Odin, the god of warriors. Another god was called Thor. He was big and jolly, with a bright red beard. He was very strong and always carried a hammer that he called Mjollni. Thor was the most popular god. We can tell this because many Vikings had lucky silver charms made in the shape of Thor's hammer. The man in the picture on page 25 making the comb is wearing a hammer charm on a chain around his neck.

HISTORY DETECTIVE

700-800	As a result of population increases in Norway, Denmark, and Sweden, farmers start looking for new land and for other ways of making a living
793	Viking raiders attack the monastery on the island of Lindisfarne, off the northeast coast of England
800	Viking settlements are established in the Orkney and Shetland Islands, off northern Scotland
810	Vikings from Denmark attack Frisia, the coastal region of what is now Germany and the Netherlands
835	A 15-year-long period of Viking raids on England begins
844	Viking raiders reach Spain, but are defeated by the Arabs in Córdoba
845	Vikings sail up the Seine River and besiege Paris
850	For the first time a party of Vikings spends the winter in England. Vikings from Sweden begin to visit Russia.
860	Norwegian Vikings find their way to Iceland. Swedish Vikings reach Istanbul.
866	A Viking "Great Army" arrives in England from Denmark. The Viking army captures York the following year.
874	Norwegian Vikings start to settle in Iceland
878	In England, King Alfred the Great defeats the Vikings. Later he allows them to settle a part of England known as the Danelaw.

893	The Vikings start raiding England again
901	Edward, king of the part of England called Wessex, starts to recapture the Danelaw
911	The king of France allows the Viking leader Rollo and his followers to settle in Normandy
954	In England, the last Viking king of York, Erik Bloodaxe, is killed at the Battle of Stainmore
980	Christianity starts to spread through the Viking homelands
985	Vikings from Iceland start to settle in Greenland
986	The Viking Bjarni Herjolfsson sees Vinland, but does not land there
991	Viking attacks on England start again
1000	Leif Eriksson sails to Vinland from Greenland
1016	The Danish Vikings win at the Battle of Ashingdon and their king, Svein Forkbeard, becomes king of England as well as Denmark. He is succeeded by his son, Canute.
1035	King Canute dies and is succeeded by his son, Harthacanute
1042	Harthacanute dies suddenly. Edward the Confessor is chosen as king of England.
1066	William, Duke of Normandy, defeats the English. He becomes king of England and the Viking raids come to an end.

GLOSSARY

afterlife: life after death

archaeologists: people who learn about life in earlier times by studying objects from the past in a careful and scientific way

artifacts: objects that have been made by people

awning: a large piece of cloth that could be used as a tent or as a cover over the deck of a ship. It was usually waterproof.

besiege: to surround a town or a building so that no one can go in or out to escape or bring supplies

byre: the building where farm animals were kept

cauldron: a large round-bottomed pan for boiling or stewing food over an open fire. It could stand on a frame called a tripod or hang from a strong chain.

chain mail: tiny rings of metal that are fastened together to make a shirt strong enough to protect the wearer from serious injury in battle

crafts workers: people who are skilled at a particular craft, for example, making jewelry

curd: the solid parts of milk that separate from the liquid when milk is heated to make cheese

Danegeld: money paid to the Vikings by the kings of England and other countries in order to be left in peace

Danelaw: the part of England in which King Alfred the Great allowed the Vikings to settle after 886. It was ruled by Viking law and included all of East Anglia and the towns of Derby, Leicester, Lincoln, Nottingham, and Stamford.

embers: the hot, glowing parts of a fire that are left when the flames die down

evidence: proof that something happened or existed

excavate: to dig up buried objects and artifacts in a scientific manner, in order to find out more about the past

flexible: easily bent

furnace: the very hot fire in which a blacksmith heats metal so that he can bend it into shape

futhark: a kind of alphabet used by the Vikings. It is named after the first six runes. These are F, U, Th, A, R and K.

grave goods: the items that were buried with a person when he or she died

hearth: the place made for a fire to burn without spreading

historians: people who learn about life in the past by studying old documents and written records

keel: the main piece of wood in the structure of a ship. It goes from end to end along the bottom of the ship.

linen: cloth made from yarn spun from fibers taken from the stem of a flax plant

longhouse: a farmhouse that got its name because of its oblong shape

madder: a wildflower with a root once used to make red dye

millstone: one of the two hard stones that were used to grind grain. They stood one on top of the other and the grain was placed in between them. They were then turned around and around by hand until the grain had been ground into flour.

monastery: a collection of buildings where monks live and practice their religion away from the rest of the world

monk: a man who lives and practices his religion in a monastery

nithing: the Viking name for someone who has broken the laws of the *thing*

outlaw: someone who has disobeyed the *thing* and so is outside the law. Outlaws were usually sent into exile. If they refused to go, anyone could kill them without risk of punishment.

raid: a violent and unexpected attack on a place. It usually included stealing property and taking people as slaves.

rapids: parts of a river with a steep descent and a very strong, fast current

ribs: the framework that holds the sides of a ship in shape

runes: the stick-like letters that make up the *futhark.* Because they were straight, they were easy to carve on wood, stone, or metal. Some Vikings thought they were magical.

sagas: stories of Viking adventures. At first the stories were learned by heart and passed on from one generation to another. Many of the stories were written down in Iceland in the 13th century.

scramasax: a large knife with one sharp edge. It was used as a weapon by the Vikings.

shift: a simple, loose-fitting dress, rather like a nightgown

Slavs: the people who were living in Russia when the Vikings arrived. The Vikings took many of them as slaves.

smithy: the building in which iron is heated so that it can be shaped into tools and weapons

spices: the seeds, roots, leaves, or fruits of certain plants used to flavor food

stocks: the strong wooden frame on which a ship is held while it is being built

thing: the local meeting of freemen, or karls, that set the laws for a particular area

traders: people who make a living by exchanging goods with other people for more goods or for money

turf: a slab of short grass with earth, bound together by the roots

Vinland: the name Leif Eriksson gave to the part of Newfoundland in which he landed. It means Vineland.

weapon smith: a metal worker who specializes in making weapons

whetstone: a very hard, smooth stone on which knife blades can be sharpened

woad: a plant that was once prized for its blue dye

INDEX